VISIONS OF WANDERLUST
THE WORLD OF TRAVEL PHOTOGRAPHY

The very best of the past two years of the *Wanderlust* Travel Photo of the Year competition

THE MAGAZINE

Wanderlust was launched in 1993 by Paul Morrison and Lyn Hughes. It has since become the UK's leading specialist travel magazine, with its hallmark mix of inspirational writing and impartial information. Top-class photography has been a feature of the magazine from the start, aiming to show the world as it is, rather than how we might like it to be.

THE PHOTO COMPETITION

The competition is launched each July and runs to the end of the year. The panel of judges draws up a shortlist of entries, which are displayed at Destinations – the UK's leading travel and holiday show. It is here that the final judging and presentations take place. Overall winners are dispatched on a photographic commission for *Wanderlust*, recent hosts being Canada and Antarctica.

For details on entering check out the August/September, October and November issues of *Wanderlust* or log on to www.wanderlust.co.uk

THANKS

The *Wanderlust* Travel Photo of the Year competition would never have become the success that it is today without the support of a number of individuals and organisations.

Destinations has provided the ideal venue every year for an exhibition of the finalists' photos, and the nerve-wracking awards ceremony. Thanks to the 'Desties' team.

Our thanks must go out to our media partners *The Independent*, and particularly senior travel editor Simon Calder, for all his encouragement and support.

We are also very grateful to the various sponsors over the past two years who have offered such excellent prizes for the competition winners, namely: Canadian Tourism Commission, Peregrine Adventures, Zoom Airlines, British Airways, Lan Airlines and Nikon.

We cannot forget, of course, the team of judges and helpers who have the unenviable task of picking the winners. And lastly, thank you to everyone who sifted through their travel shots and entered their best ones into the competition. To those who made it into this book, congratulations. To those who didn't, we hope you'll be inspired and try again next year.

Contents

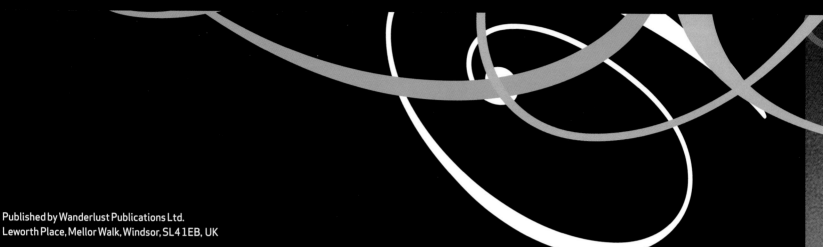

Published by Wanderlust Publications Ltd.
Leworth Place, Mellor Walk, Windsor, SL4 1EB, UK

Tel: +44 (0)1753 620426
Fax: +44 (0)1753 620474

www.wanderlust.co.uk
www.goWander.com
Email: info@wanderlust.co.uk

Editor-in-Chief/Publisher: Lyn Hughes
Editor: Dan Linstead
Art Director: Graham Berridge
Editorial: Sarah Baxter, Paul Bloomfield, Sarah Kiernan, Lizzie Matthews
Picture Editor: Amy Bellew
Operations Director: Danny Callaghan

ISBN 978-0-9540926-3-4
Printed in China by 1010 Printing International
Printed 2007

**This book is dedicated to
Paul Morrison (1958-2004)**

Welcome to the third *Visions of Wanderlust* – a showcase of some of the top entries in the *Wanderlust* Travel Photo of the Year Competition of the past two years.

In setting up the competition we wanted to capture the sense of discovery that real travellers experience on real trips. These shots aren't set up, don't use paid models and haven't been days or weeks in the making. They've been taken on everything from cheap happy-snappy cameras upwards. Yet despite this, time and time again people comment on the quality, saying that they can't believe the photos haven't been taken by professionals.

The competition started in 1996 in response to the high standard of photographs that we were receiving for our regular competitions in the magazine. It rapidly became the largest travel photography competition for amateurs in the UK, culminating in a major exhibition each year at Destinations Holiday & Travel Show.

We published the first *Visions of Wanderlust* in 2001. Much has happened since then. There were no digital images included in the first book, whereas around three-quarters of the images in this book were taken on digital cameras. And each year we've had the great digital debate – if a photo has been manipulated is it a true travel image? We've decided that we'll excude mainipulated images – surely a great travel photograph is about capturing a moment, not creating it?

Sadly, since the first book was published, my partner/husband/soulmate Paul Morrison has died. Paul was passionate about travel, passionate about photography, and without him there would be no *Wanderlust* Travel Photo of the Year competition and no *Visions*, either. I hope you get as much pleasure from the superb images in this book as he would have done.

Lyn

Lyn Hughes, Editor-in-Chief/Publisher

1 in the wild

Orangutan, Gunung Leuser National Park, Sumatra, Indonesia

"Volunteering with the Orangutan Health Project in Sumatra gave me a fantastic opportunity to photograph these amazing primates in their natural environment. The Sumatran orangutan subspecies is even more critically endangered than its better-known cousin in Borneo. This one was near a feeding station in Gunung Leuser National Park, staring towards the encroaching palm oil plantation a few miles away. I just had time for a couple of shots before he swung away into the trees." *Mark Corti*

Cheetah smile, Masai Mara, Kenya

"Returning from watching the wildebeest crossing the
Mara River, I came upon this female cheetah fast
asleep on a termite mound. Not wishing to disturb her,
I attached a long-distance lens and waited. After five
minutes she opened her eyes, gave me a quick glance
and then ignored me to let me know she was in total
control. Finally, raising her head, she stretched,
yawned and gave me a beautiful smile." *Chris Levan*

Brown bear, Brook Falls, Alaska, USA

"I was going on an organised trip to Alaska, so I tacked on a visit to Katmai National Park for a week of camping, hiking and watching the brown bears before I joined the tour. This gave me the chance to get up close (sometimes too close) and personal to photograph the bears fishing." *James Sprawson*

Back down to earth –
cheetah cub,
Masai Mara, Kenya

"Before this photo was taken, this
cheetah cub, together with its mother
and five siblings, had snacked on
a hare washed down with a welcome
drink from a muddy puddle. One of the
playful cubs then decided to climb
a tree. Cheetahs are not renowned as
climbers, but it seems no one had
bothered to tell this cub; it only
managed to scale to a height of about
2m before deciding to come back
down to earth and rejoin its family in
search of a more substantial meal."
Tony Costa

Vona Vona Lagoon, Lola Island, Solomon Islands

"I was enjoying a weekend of fishing on Lola Island, away from rotations at the local hospital in Munda. While attempting to reach a nearby island by canoe I was forced to discard my dugout on a sandbar. Catching sight of several fishermen, I walked over and exchanged greetings. In moments they handed over their catch, suggesting I take it back for a barbecue. Standing alone in the ankle-deep waters, gripping the vibrantly painted crayfish, I watched these generous strangers depart and realised that this moment defined the emotions I had sought through travel in the Western Provinces." *Nicholas Dawe*

Lions on the hunt near Okonjima, Namibia

"We were in Namibia for three weeks, including a two-week safari and a visit to the AfriCat Foundation at Okonjima. This fantastic organisation rescues and rehabilitates leopards and cheetahs, which we tracked in Land Rovers and on foot. It was about 5pm when we saw a couple of older lions starting to look for their evening meal. They came very close and the sun was getting low. One of the lions stopped in a nice pool of light, let out an unbelievably low, rumbling roar, and gave my wife a rather worrying look." *Rik Walton*

Monal pheasant, Nepal

"Usually I press my delete button almost as much as my shutter clicks. When I go to Nepal, though, opportunities and ideas seem to present themselves everywhere. I enjoyed this one, crouching and shooting through and around branches with a heavy but manageable lens." *Paul Marshall*

Elephants with Mount Kilimanjaro, Amboseli National Park, Kenya

"These elephants were part of a larger family group making their daily trek from the foothills of Kilimanjaro to the marshlands of Amboseli. It was a stunning April morning and all the elephants in the area were heading for the cooling waters of the national park, where they spent the day feeding before returning to the lower reaches of the mountain for the evening." *Andrew Macey*

Elephant seal with king penguins, Gold Harbour, South Georgia

"During my short visit I was overwhelmed by the sight of king penguins and elephant seals. To me, the two species typified South Georgia and I wanted a shot of both together. I saw this seal lying at the edge of the surf, snot dribbling down his chin, and a parade of penguins that would soon pass in front of him. I dropped to the ground and used my bag as a tripod, selecting a wide depth of field as I wanted both in focus. By the time I'd taken the shot I had a penguin chick pecking at me and my legs were covered in guano but I am happy with the result." *Phil Crosby*

Napoleon wrasse, Daedalus Reef, Red Sea, Egypt

"The Napoleon wrasse is one of my favourite coral reef fish because of its impressive size, beautiful appearance and friendly disposition. I encountered this one in a cave and took care not to disturb him. Later in the dive, I found that he had followed me! It was then that I took this photograph, at a depth of 8m." *Terence Dormer*

Snowy egret by a waterfall, El Salton, Cuba

"Settling down to enjoy a picnic at a small, waterfall-fed lake in El Salton, I noticed this snowy egret circling above us. To my surprise, it landed next to the waterfall on the opposite side of the lake. I grabbed my camera and rushed barefoot over many slippery rocks to get this shot." *Michael Dalhousie*

Lion cub on mum, Masai Mara, Kenya

"Lions are quite widespread in the Mara but all too frequently they are seen fast asleep – they rest up to 19 hours a day. We'd left at 5am and, literally minutes before the sun rose, we found a pride of around 15 lions near the Ol Kiombo area of the reserve. This mother had three cubs and, despite the early lighting conditions, I was determined to use slow film.For a moment this young one perched on mum, a lovely shade line bisected them and sumptuous light illuminated the proceedings. This shot highlighted the wonderful relationship between mum and cub and also the fantastic light that East Africa offers."
Paul Goldstein

Polar bear cubs, Spitsbergen, Norway

"For any journey to this part of the world, polar bears are the wildlife Grail. For the previous two days a pea-soup fog had descended on the ship and made excursions impossible. This shot was taken during a magical time around midnight, when most passengers had gone to bed (we woke them). The cubs were following their mother and she had already made the jump, checking the take-off point first. The conditions were demanding and the light poor, but I like the comical side to the shot and also the genuine wild feel, as we were many kilometres from the shore." *Paul Goldstein*

Lions mating, Etosha, Namibia

"This shot was taken during the early hours of a November morning in Namibia when what is regarded as a private affair quickly became public. I tried to capture the moment with passion and respect. To achieve a great wildlife shot, I needed to be ready for anything – and I was! The lions were going through the emotions of mating and the shot was taken just after the male had released his bite from the female and let out an unforgettable loud roar." *Glenda Skidmore*

Le Conte Bay, Inside Passage, Alaska, USA

"We had already been in the rubber dinghy for six hours, sailing around the floating icebergs in Le Conte Bay, Alaska. Time passed quickly as we enjoyed and photographed the beautiful shapes and the incredible shades of blue in the icebergs. We were about to return to the yacht when, in the distance, we noticed an amazing iceberg with a perforated outline like Swiss cheese. As we drew closer we were struck by its size and beauty. To perfect the picture the sun came out from behind the clouds and lit the berg from behind – a wonderful, unforgettable moment." *Danny Hadas*

A mother watches helplessly,
Masai Mara, Kenya

"Sometimes the realities of natural selection can be
a bit harsh. This young gazelle fawn had been 'hidden'
in the grass by its mother. Foolishly, she opted to
conceal her offspring among a pride of lions. This
lioness virtually stumbled across the fawn, and the
inevitable scene was played out." *Chris Windram*

Karakul Lake on the Karakoram Highway, Xinjiang, China

"Following the Silk Road across China, I found myself on the Karakoram Highway at 3,600m. The High Pamir plateau is punctuated by this single, vivid patch of blue/green, and we were walking round it when a family of Kyrgyz nomads invited us to stay the night in their yurt. The next morning I awoke to this sensational view – the only sound was one of the family's yearling camels letting out repeated guttural cries. For a few moments there was a touching, isolated poignancy to the scene. Shortly after I took this photo, a pair of adult camels appeared to reassure the youngster and the landscape reverted to silence."
Robin Meldrum

Snow petrel, icefields near Portal Point, Antarctic Peninsula

"We were cruising in a Zodiac when our guide spotted a pair of snow petrels. One wandered into a position where it was framed perfectly, with good light and a contrasting backdrop. To me, this shot captures both the stark nature of the Antarctic environment and the beauty that survives there." *Phil Crosby*

Lounging leopard, Ulusaba Private Game Reserve, South Africa

"The 5.30am wake-up call was unnecessary – we'd already been rudely awoken by baboons mating on the thatched roof! Two swaying rope bridges later we reached the game lodge for a quick bite and a cuppa, before clambering into the open-topped Land Rover. Our guides, Duard and Anton, took us close to a magnificent male elephant, before an even closer encounter with lionesses and cubs from the buffalo-killing 'southern pride'. The morning highlight was this beautiful female leopard, high in a tree, complete with a steenbok – her recent kill."

Rodney Woods

Red colobus monkey, Jozani Forest, Zanzibar, Tanzania

"I went to Jozani Forest to see a rare species of red colobus monkey endemic
to the island – one of the most endangered species of monkey in the world.
I followed a crowd of them crashing recklessly through the forest canopy
with squeaks of alarm and, when they stopped to eat leaves, my chance
came to photograph them. I was particularly interested in the crown of long
white hair that fans out around the face. The one in this photo came down
to eat some charcoal (which helps with digestion). Kneeling on the ground
I managed to take its photo as it was looking up." *Marie-Laure Stone*

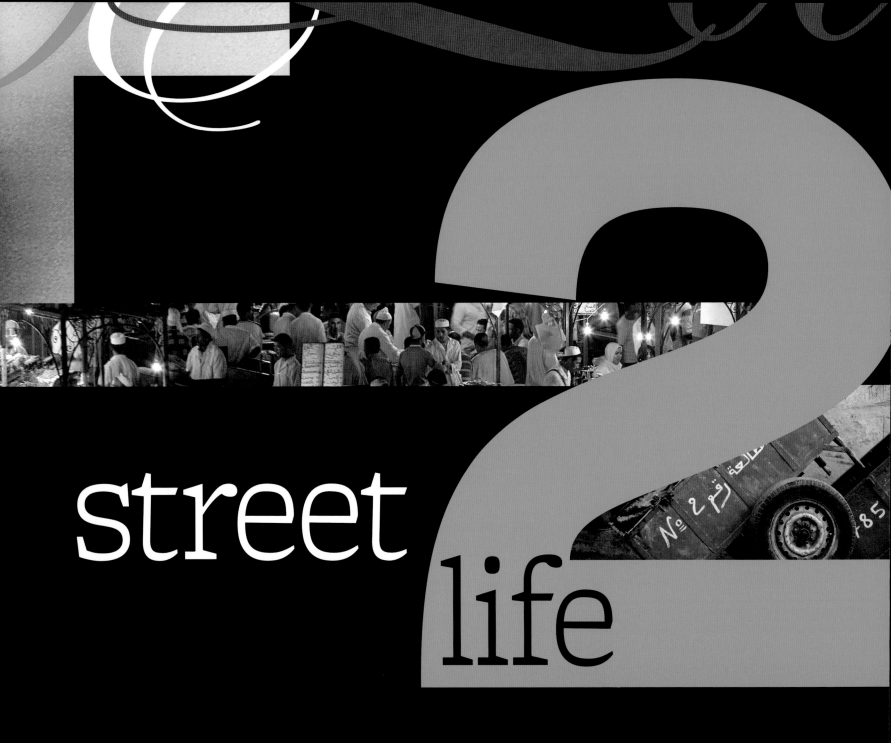

street life

Tea break, Marrakesh, Morocco

"A lone cart worker sips traditional mint tea as he takes a break from shifting heavy goods around the busy souks in Marrakesh. Most carts consist of a simple metal bucket welded to old car wheels, which can be either pushed or pulled by hand. Small enough to fit down crowded alleys, these humble carts are crucial in resupplying traders with stock, moving heavy suitcases or simply clearing waste at the end of the day." *Ralph Barnett*

Street kids, Yunnan, China

"This photo was taken in September 2006 at Menghun market in Xishuangbanna, Yunnan Province. The boys were playing around on the street together. I let them play with my camera for a while (they loved looking through the viewfinder); after that, they didn't mind me taking their photo."
Heidi Laughton

Cuban cowboy, Trinidad, Cuba

"During a return visit to the Unesco World Heritage site of Trinidad we were walking around the town trying to give out some prints to the people we had photographed six months earlier. We met a group of cowboys who, when they were not working on the farm, made a bit of extra money by taking tourists out riding." *Janet Edwards*

Shade bathing, Copacabana, Lake Titicaca, Bolivia

"This shot was captured in the midday heat of Copacabana. All the locals wear full indigenous dress, with only the rim of their hats offering shade, so people move at a slow pace. When I rounded the street corner I saw this lady leaning back into the shade of the wall. The interesting graffiti and her pose caught my eye and seemed to capture a perfect example of Bolivian street life." *Tessa Emery*

Bringing home the bacon, Alausi, Ecuador

"This photograph was taken in the Ecuadorian town of Alausi as a few men and women returned from the market with their animals. The woman pictured broke off from the others and as she passed me by I found the scene quite hypnotic – the pig shuffling proudly ahead and its owner struggling to keep a rein."
Alison O'Meara

Watching life go by on Chandni Chowk, Old Delhi, India

"Chandni Chowk bazaar in Old Delhi is always a throng of people, being one of the largest wholesale and retail markets in the world. At the mid-point is the Gurudwara Sis Ganj Sikh temple, where one is welcome to escape the commotion for a while. From the roof, the sight of all those people is amazing. I wanted to capture this against the context of a local who was placidly observing the comings and goings below."
Dr Philip Lawson

Djemaa el-Fna Square at night, Marrakesh, Morocco

"One of the most captivating sights in Marrakesh is that of the snake charmers, storytellers and acrobats that perform in the Djemaa el-Fna square. The colours, smells, smoke and sounds easily draw you in." *Gerald Spice*

Wheelbarrow boys, San'a, Yemen

"This photo was taken while I was wandering around the old part of San'a close to the souk. Walking down a narrow bustling street, I came across the 'wheelbarrow boys'. They all work for the shop next to them in the photo, which I think sold fabric. Between deliveries they lounge in the wheelbarrows, talking and chewing *qat*. I didn't want to intrude, so I took just a few shots."
Raphael Schutzer-Weissmann

Too many cooks, Djemaa el-Fna, Marrakesh, Morocco

"Although the area is now more tourist-orientated, scenes like this have been taking place for hundreds of years; I tried to get a flavour of the square as it would have been seen over the generations." *Gerald Spice*

Cycling to work, Kenya

"Early in the morning, following an overnight storm, we had stopped to photograph a family of hyenas in the Masai Mara. I noticed three Maasai cycling along the track in the distance; the contrast between the colourful Maasai clothing and the still-stormy sky in the morning light really caught my eye." *Alan Fretten*

landscape

Enys Dodnan, Land's End, UK

"As evening arrived at Land's End and the light levels dropped, an approaching storm battered the coast with fierce winds. Long after all the tourists had left I remained alone on the clifftops, standing as close to the edge as I dared, to photograph the tempestuous water crashing around the ancient sea stack Enys Dodnan." *Adam Burton*

Rice paddies, Nepal

"Returning from the Annapurna Sanctuary, trekking towards Pokhara we
stayed in a local teahouse. There was a tremendous storm overnight, with
torrential rain that beat down deafeningly on the corrugated-iron roof.
The rain had stopped the following morning, leaving beautiful clear air, and
when the sun came up it created a wonderful quality of light and colour."
Alan Fretten

Ta Prohm, Angkor, Cambodia

"Ta Prohm is a 12th-century Buddhist temple
that was once home to more than 70,000
people, including high priests, monks,
assistants, dancers and labourers. It was
rediscovered in 1860 by a French naturalist,
Henri Mouhot, and has largely been left the way
he found it. The ancient structures are still
gripped by massive strangler fig and banyan
tree roots, giving visitors the feeling
of discovering an archaeological site for the
first time." *Martin Chamberlain*

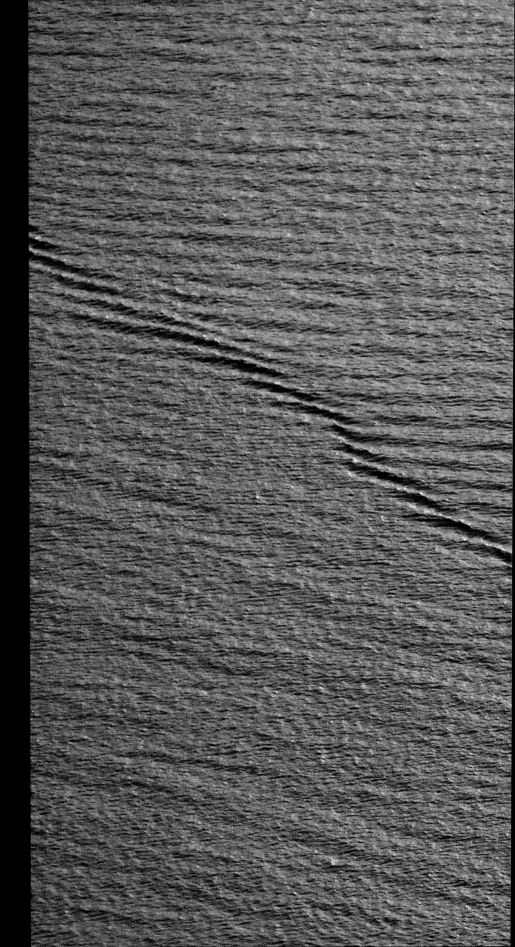

Golden wake, Santorini, Greece

"Having just arrived on Santorini Island, I witnessed
the most amazing golden sunset I had ever seen.
There was a mist over the sea that was diffusing the
light and creating a golden glow in the atmosphere.
Straight away, I went to the edge of the cliffs to
capture this stunning light show. Looking down,
I saw this lone fishing boat coming in for the evening.
I loved the texture created by the combination of the
boat's wake, the ripple of the ocean waves and the
golden light." *Carly Anderson*

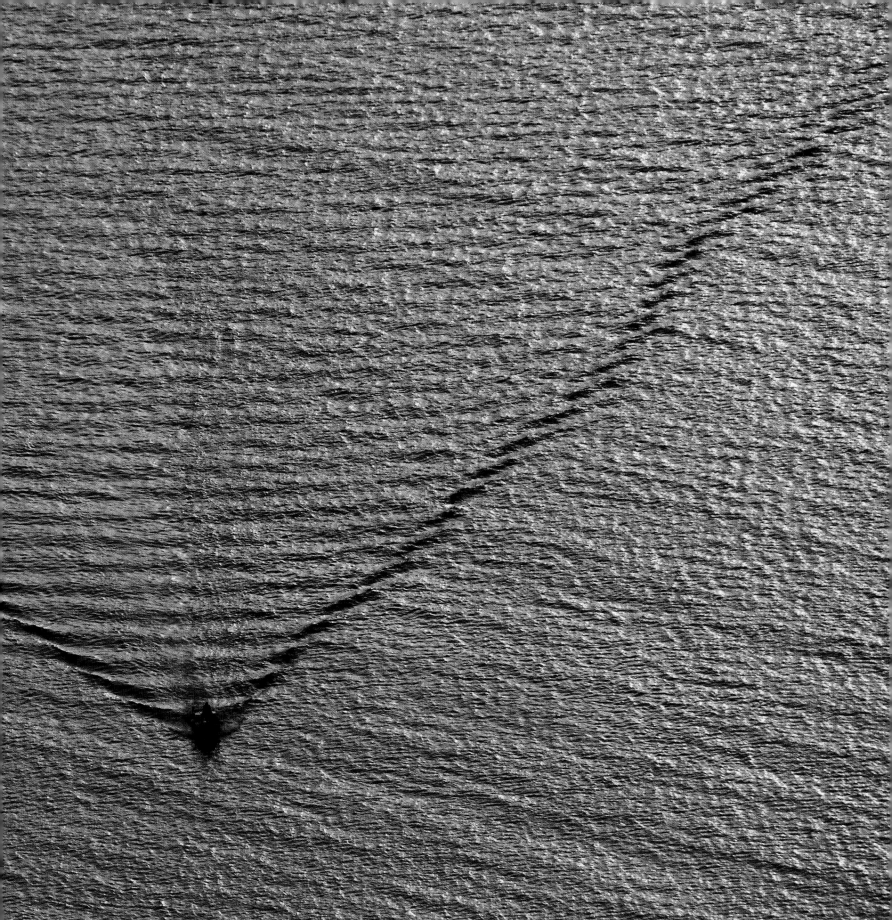

Black Rock Cottage, Rannoch Moor, Scotland

"This picture of Black Rock Cottage was taken in March 2006. As far as possible, I like my landscapes to be true reproductions of the conditions experienced on the day. In pre-dawn temperatures of around –10°C, I waited to capture the summit of Buachaille Etive Mor bathed in the warmth of the first morning light." *Gloria Malton*

Iceberg wave, Antarctica

"In December 2005 we were approaching Graham Land through a heavy South Atlantic swell. We had just passed Elephant Island, famous for its key role in the 1914-16 Shackleton expedition. The rolling waves hitting this huge iceberg were almost exploding, as if smashing into solid land. The dark, savage sea in the foreground and the stunning and magical scenery of Antarctica behind came together to create an unforgettable, once-in-a-lifetime experience." *Eddy Lane*

High above the dunes, Namibia

"Seeing the dunes of the Namib Desert from the sky is a truly stunning experience. You can see small dunes forming strange patterns and huge dunes sculptured by winds from the nearby sea. So are these big or small? It's up to you to decide." *Frederic Mottier*

Fragile desert, near Swakopmund, Namibia

"I found this piece of litter in the dunes near Swakopmund on a recent trip to Namibia and thought the 'Fragile' label ironic."

Kevin Davis

At the summit of Blencathra, Lake District, UK

"It was February when we decided to climb Halls Fell to the summit of Blencathra. The first shoulder was easy, but Halls Fell ridge was a whole different ball game. The weather had closed in; snow showers were frequent, with gusty winds. It was dizzying, exciting and rewarding to finally reach the plateau where the image was taken, viewing the broad summit of Blencathra. The sun shone between showers of snow – a photographer's paradise, not to be forgotten." *Ron Tear*

Troll's Ladder, Norway

"The Troll's Ladder is one of the most spectacular roads in the world. Running between Valldal and Åndalsnes in Norway's northern fjords, it was completed in 1936 after eight years' construction and is closed during the winter. This photograph shows some of the road's 11 hairpin bends and the Stigfossen waterfall." *Martin Chamberlain*

people

Otavalo market, Ecuador

"Otavalo is well known for its lively Saturday market, which caters for locals and tourists alike. It was this variety that interested me most about the place. I walked off the beaten track for a while and came across this side street wall mural, celebrating the traditional Quechua way of life. I set up my tripod low and close to the wall and ushered people past as I crouched in the gutter. For me, the shot is all about movement and change – how in these times of rapid development, the local Quechua have achieved commercial success while still holding on to their rich cultural heritage." *Ben Haskey*

Children in the mist, Missouri Botanical Garden, St Louis, USA

"This photo was taken on a hot, steamy evening during an open-air jazz concert in the Missouri Botanical Garden. The children were cooling down in a specially erected steam tent and were backlit by the setting sun. I waited until the decisive moment before tripping the shutter to get the perfect pose."

Danny Beath

Horse rider, Mongolia

"From out of nowhere, the horseman emerged. As in the time of Genghis Khan, horseback riding is a fundamental part of Mongolian daily life and remains the main mode of travel across the country's vast plains. The world's most sparsely populated nation, Mongolia is also the only country where people are outnumbered by horses." *Richard Tabaka*

Jaipur leg, India

"I had walked this street many times in the old city and seen this paan wala in exactly the same position every day, his one foot rested upon his Jaipur leg. Today was different, however – a mirror had appeared overnight as if by magic, a photographic opportunity not to be missed. In the city where the Jaipur leg, a low-cost prosthetic, was invented, he proved the perfect model."

David Dunning

Blue boy, Orissa, India

"Behind a ramshackle cluster of market stalls an impromptu *Demsa* dance was in full swing. The Gadaba women danced in semicircles while the men played musical instruments. Suddenly, the crowd stopped clapping and chanting. A young man, his face painted a vivid blue, stood in the middle of the circle. He vanished into the multitude, only to reappear like a deity on the shoulders of two men. The dancing started again with the banging of drums and joyful singing, as he was spun in a circle to the delight of the participants." *Kieron Nelson*

Cormorant fishing, Guangxi, China

"Trained cormorants are used to catch fish by night in Guangxi. Powerful lights attract huge numbers of insects, which in turn attract fish to feed. The birds' necks are ringed to prevent them eating their catch. Every seventh catch, the birds' owner releases the ring to allow them a reward – at least, that's the received wisdom. I couldn't see how they could keep count with up to half a dozen birds on each small boat." *John Pennock*

Mountain high tea, Hunza, Pakistan

"After a four-hour hike through the valley of the looming Ultar Nala in Hunza, north Pakistan, we were presented with a lush meadow of fairytale perfection. In need of some refreshment, we were fortunate enough to be greeted by a group of shepherds. One invited us to share tea and apricots fresh from the valley; unfortunately, but to the amusement of us all, with this spirit of generosity he had accidentally added a pound of salt to the tea instead of sugar!" *Kate Malone*

Children meet in Nairobi, Kenya

The David Sheldrick Trust is a charity dedicated to the raising of orphaned baby elephants and rhinos. It also runs an education programme for local schools, and a class of Kenyan primary school children had come to visit at feeding time. A small number of tourists, including this toddler, were also present. This photo was a candid, spur-of-the-moment shot that captured the expressions of the children as they met. Within a few seconds the children's attention had reverted back to the animals."
Dr James Haeney

Catnapping with the catch, Burma (Myanmar)

"On a hot November morning I took a stroll across the rickety, 200-year-old U Bein's Bridge. As a fisherwoman slowly drifted out beneath us, sunlight caught the silvery metallic fish scales, which sparkled like diamonds in the bottom of the boat. Lying flat on my stomach, I carefully shuffled forward to the edge directly above her. With a direct drop of 30ft, plus the constant unsteady movement of the bridge as people passed by, it's amazing I managed to capture a sharp image before she hauled the boat back into the shadows." *Paul Strawson*

Old man looking at lanterns, Yasukuni Shrine, Tokyo, Japan

"Of all Tokyo's shrines, Yasukuni is the most controversial. It was built to honour the dead of Japan's wars, and every July the colourful Mitama Matsuri ('soul festival') is held to remember them. Surviving family members pay for a lantern carrying the name of the fallen serviceman; then, like this old man, they spend a quiet moment with those they've lost as the chaos of the festival continues around them." *Damon Coulter*

Flirty fun, Sancti Spíritus, Cuba

"This was one of those infamous 'last photo opportunities of the day',
where the last photo is the one you've been waiting for. There seemed to
be a lovely little bit of Hispanic flirting going on. The scene was so simple,
but captivating and touching. I only had a moment to whip out my camera
equipment before he moved away. No time for composition or light
monitoring, so when I saw the result I was delighted that I had my reward.
I hope the *hombre* in the photo got his reward too!" *Antony Stanton*

Meeting Mr Khan, near Agra, India

"We stopped for a visit at the deserted Mughal city of Fatehpur Sikri. Sameer, our leader, warned us of the eccentricity of the elderly local guide, Mr Khan, who would lecture us like schoolkids. And he was right! In an authoritarian manner, Mr Khan told of the mosques, palaces and forts, and – to ensure we gave him our full attention – he asked us questions at the end. It was a real joy to meet Mr Khan. Despite being more than 80 years old, he retained his enthusiasm, and the sparkle in his eyes is well reflected in this portrait." *Elsbeth Linhoff*

Asmat boy, near Agats, West Papua

"The Asmat were once the most feared tribe in New Guinea. The rare arrival of a handful of tourists gives the whole village an excuse to dress up and re-enact a warrior dance. Inside the communal long house, this boy's striking face paint and cassowary headdress caught my eye. He seemed proud that I'd picked him out to photograph." *Jonathan Clay*

Pleneau Island, Antarctica

"We all sat silently on the edge of our boat, listening to the sound of its engine stopping and starting as we cut our way through the sea ice. We knew this was the penultimate day before turning around and heading north, and as the temperature dropped and the sun began to set, everyone took in a breath and looked around in awe. Each of us was in their own separate world. That is the only way you can explain Antarctica – it is another world." *Kirsty Denley*

Apatani grandmother, Arunachal Pradesh, India

"Enticed by a generous supply of tobacco, this shy, elderly Apatani woman told a story of customs and rituals that are in decline or have been eliminated entirely. As a sign of tribal allegiance and beauty, both her nostrils were pierced at an early age to allow the insertion of the dark-coloured circular cane. She also endured the rudimentary tattooing of blue and black stripes running vertically down from the forehead, over the bridge of the nose to the chin. This was to protect her from evil spirits." *Kieron Nelson*

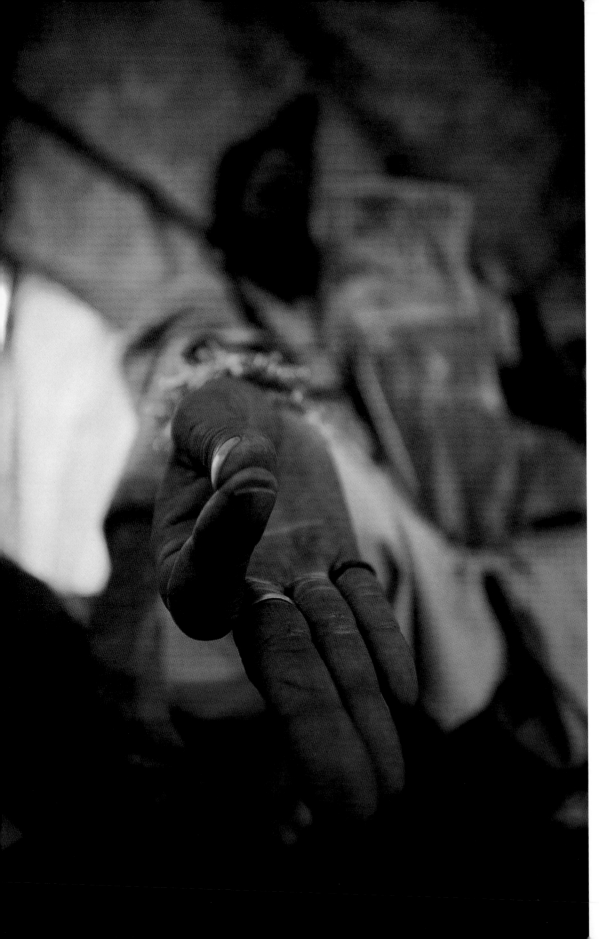

Shrine and sadhu, Varanasi, India

"I'd woken at first light to wander along the ghats, and gone upriver to the calmer fringes of the city in search of a little peace. There, on a small spit of sand, a devotee of Shiva had constructed a temporary dwelling and shrine of bowed branches and saffron-coloured sheets. The shrine was full of holy objects and, at its centre, sat the most tranquil and welcoming of holy men. Both shrine and sadhu had a peaceful yet strangely purposeful feel. This image was my attempt to capture something of this feeling." *Jeremy Bishop*

Solitude at Sera Monastery, Tibet

Once or twice a day, 120 monks form small groups in the main yard of this monastery to argue theological matters. Each monk claps his hands at the end of every phrase, while leaning forward to his audience. I took a lot of pictures, but felt that this strange spectacle couldn't be reproduced on film. Suddenly, among the crowd and noise, I noticed a lone woman praying quietly behind a half-open door. I liked the idea of opposition between the stillness of the woman and the movement of the pendulum-like door knocker, adding an impression of time slowing down." *Ioannis Lykouris*

Reflections of San'a, Yemen

"My first impression of Yemen wasn't the best – I spent the first three hours persuading the immigration officers to let me into the country – but after that, all was fantastic. I fell in love with the capital, Sana'a, especially its old quarter: beautifully decorated houses, colourful markets, gorgeous mosques and, above all, its people – always smiling and hospitable. There was a man selling mirrors in one of the old city's bazaars. I caught the reflections of the passers-by and took about 20 shots. This one seemed like a typical image of the Yemeni people – men wearing white-red scarves, veiled women and the ever-cheeky kids." *Petr Hruska*

Nyangatom shepherd boy, Omo Valley, Ethiopia

"In the southern Omo Valley, home of the Nyangatom tribe, you cannot help but be struck by the scarcity and necessity of water. A shepherd boy will wander all day in the searing heat, only bringing his animals to a well for a drink before nightfall. Plastic bottles brought in and discarded by tourists are highly prized possessions." *Jonathan Clay*

Fisher boy,
Karachi, Pakistan

"In Karachi's golden, late afternoon sun, a small group of fishermen using traditional cast nets were making end-of-day attempts to increase their catch. The gods were shining on the landscape and lighting but not the fishermen, and the dignified stoicism of this boy hides the sadness of a two-fish day."

Kate Malone

journey **5**

Tuareg and camel, Aïr Mountains, Sahara Desert, Niger

"My first encounter with the mysterious 'Blue Men of the Sahara' was under a moonless sky, at the only well available for several days. As we left I bemoaned the fact that my photographic endeavours would now be concentrated on the landscape. Then, at sunrise, I spotted three silhouetted figures crossing the dunes on camel back. My guide smiled and told me she had arranged a special encounter with the men we had met at the well, and hoped I would be happy. Thoughts of disappointment were now a distant memory, as I prepared my camera for the arrival of the Tuareg." *Kieron Nelson*

Parque Nacional Lauca, near Putre, Chile

"This image depicts the high Andes altiplano, including the
6,348m Parinacota volcano, which we intended to climb. I was
keen to capture this stunning landscape and, despite suffering
from the altitude, persevered to steady a mini tripod on the
spongy surface to obtain maximum depth of field and capture the
detail of the unusual foreground." *Chris Evans*

Camel Fair, Pushkar, Rajasthan, India

"This picture was taken at the Camel Fair, which is held on the first full moon in November at Pushkar, on the edge of the Thar Desert in Rajasthan. A group of traders was resting after travelling from all areas of the state to sell their camels." *Pauline Horton*

Somewhere on the
Andean Plateau, Peru

"This shot was taken on the PeruRail
train on the way to Cusco and Machu
Picchu, my ultimate destination.
After leaving Puno's markets, the
train started its long, slow, colourful
journey upwards. Within hours we
reached the Andean mountains. The
scenery was fantastic – huts were
scattered along the tracks, and
every so often I'd spot a vicuña or an
alpaca. There was plenty of time to
take pictures and plenty of time
to experiment: here is the result."
Christine Moinard

Turtle heading out to sea, Floreana, the Galápagos Islands

"Post Office Bay, on the island of Floreana, is famous for its barrel, placed there by whalers in 1793 so that post could be dropped off and collected by other vessels. These days it is used by tourists to send postcards home. The bay is a snorkelling paradise and a breeding ground for Pacific green turtles. This magnificent individual had been feeding on sea grass in the shallow water. As he swam back out to the open ocean he surfaced to breathe, allowing us to capture this image of turtle, island and our yacht, the *MV San José*."

Dr James Haeney

Dune above
Dead Vlei, Nambia

"Climbing sand dunes is the most exhausting form of exercise I've ever undertaken, so I paused to have a rest with the excuse of taking a photo. The shadows of the people in front of me and their footsteps made a nice picture against the sharp silhouette of the dune crest above. As we proceeded (two steps forward, one step back) the summit didn't seem to get any nearer but I was determined not to hold up the younger people behind me. Eventually we were rewarded with a magnificent view of the weird and eerie Dead Vlei below."
Jill Toman

Monks' feet, Chiang Mai, Thailand

"I asked our guide where I could photograph monks and, while everyone else stayed in bed, he and I ended up outside a hilltop temple in the pouring rain at six o'clock in the morning. At first I was disappointed by the rain, but I persevered with the help of our taxi driver, who took me under his wing – and his umbrella! When I saw the results I was so pleased, because the reflections of the robes gave another dimension to the picture. Seeing the monks' bare feet on the slippery road reminded me of their sacrifices and humility as they go about their ritual journey."

Celia Mannings

action 6

Salt fields near
Nha Trang, Vietnam

"We left Nha Trang at first light, arriving
at the salt fields around 6.30am. It was
already baking hot, yet the workers were
covered from head to foot, some even
wearing long socks, as they trudged across
the fields carrying heavy baskets. I shot
several rolls of film over two hours or so,
and this image was definitely my favourite
from the morning." *Lisa Mardell*

Market scene, Manica, Mozambique

"My wife and I were on an arduous journey from southern Mozambique to Malawi. After 12 torturous hours stuffed in a tin can on wheels, we finally stopped in Manica. We had a couple of hours before sunset to explore the dusty marketplace. The scene was bathed in a beautiful crisp light, with splashes of colour among the chaos. When my eye caught the colourful beer advert, I thought it would make a great backdrop for the myriad cyclists passing by. I waded through the traffic and panned the cyclists. The locals were left wondering what I was up to, and I walked away with my favourite image of the trip." *Darryl Monson*

Horses of the Camargue, France

"I went to the Camargue last April specifically to photograph its famous white horses. Although they used to run wild they are now rarely seen, so we were taken to a ranch where they are bred, their bloodlines kept pure, and where they are used to round up the black 'fighting' bulls of the area. They are thought to be descended from prehistoric horses that lived more than 17,000 years ago; now, they have adapted to the area's wetlands and salt marshes. They are so strong it is said they are able to canter through mud up to their bellies." *Gloria Cotton*

Hiwatari Festival, Mount Takao, Japan

"This Buddhist fire-walking festival at Mount Takao, near Tokyo, is a photographers' dream. Unfortunately there are lots of other photographers in Japan. Somehow I managed to talk myself into the professional enclosure. This shot was taken from the crowd – just after the monks had finished their walk across the fire, ordinary people can join in. This tiny little old lady praying devotedly as she is helped across the coals by a huge monk seemed to say so much about the festival." *Damon Coulter*

Action on the Yangzi, China

"Our cruise ship, *Princess Elaine*, entered the Wu Gorge of the great Yangzi River mid-morning, from where a ferryman took us up the Shennong River to a waiting flotilla of 'pea pod' boats. The pilots of these boats came from the local mountain tribe and their barely existent footwear intrigued me. I jumped into the first one to sit next to the captain. As the water became shallow and rapid, the captain set aside his paddle and took up a bamboo pole in one hand and the rudder in the other. His expression of strength and effort – giving every last drop to get that boat upstream – was amazing." *Dr KK Aravind*

Traditional fishing boat, Hoi An, Vietnam

"I had taken a water taxi from the centre of Hoi An to a restaurant located out in the estuary. The driver was in no rush and was happy to detour as we came across brightly coloured boats, shrimp nets and local fishermen. Then, out of nowhere, appeared a small local boat being rowed by a Vietnamese woman in her traditional conical hat, carrying a wizened man casting his net. The driver was good enough to position the boat for me and ask if it was OK to photograph the fisherman. The great thing about digital was the look on their faces when they saw the shot on the screen."

Jon Bunston

Fisherman throwing net, Kerala, India

"I am from Kerala and have seen fishermen throw nets since I was a child; I have also seen boring pictures of it, so I wanted to take it from a different viewpoint. I got hold of these fishermen and told them my idea: for me to get into the water neck-deep and for them to throw the net over me. The idea was to get a fish's view of a cast net. The problem was that the net had lead balls all around it and, unless their throw was perfect, one of these could whack me on the head. The first two days we tried this, the weather was bad but on the third day, just after sunset, the sky cleared and I got the shot." *Dr Mani Puthuran*

Peanut ladies outside Banjul, Gambia

"Driving towards Banjul, we saw women standing on hills, repeatedly pouring something from buckets. I just had to go in with my camera, and photographer Glenn Edwards, who organised the trip, obviously felt the same. In moments his smiled had gained us permission. It turned out the women were shelling peanuts, and the hills were thousands of peanut husks. They were a joy to photograph, laughing and joking, delighting in covering us with husks and dust. We were no doubt a novel distraction from what must have been back-breaking, never-ending work." *Celia Mannings*

Novice monks enjoying Kuang Si waterfalls, Laos

"After trekking in Laos, my friend and I felt we deserved a day of relaxation at the Kuang Si waterfalls – a series of small pools tumbling down a steep cliff. I had just dived into the icy waters when a group of novice monks burst out of the bushes. Monkhood in Laos is certainly no barrier to fun and I couldn't believe my eyes when they started shimmying up a tree and throwing themselves into the pool below. I scrambled over the rocks to my camera and balanced myself precariously beside the pool to gain the ideal position. I was petrified that I would slip but it was well worth it to get this photo." *Jane Lockett*

Errera Channel, off the coast of Cuverville Island, Antarctica

"For our honeymoon, my wife and I took a whistle-stop tour around the world, the highlight being a cruise to the Antarctic Peninsula. On our penultimate day we were awoken at 6am to the kind of day you might only get once a season – there wasn't a cloud in the sky and the ocean was a perfect mirror. While taking a Zodiac cruise through a sea of icebergs, we found ourselves being followed by a colony of porpoising gentoo penguins. Getting the shot was tricky – by the time you had seen them they'd gone. I had to aim at the last splash and hope another would follow." *Douglas Nesbit*

Dancing corn, Udaipur, Rajasthan, India

"I travelled into the hills outside Udaipur on a scooter with an Indian man who wanted to show me his village. On the way we came across this small hamlet where children were playing outside in a courtyard. They came running towards us, grabbed my hands and took me into the courtyard where two women in beautiful saris were sieving corn that had been roasting in the sun. The dust from the corn twinkled in the sunlight as the women shook the steel bowls. I could have stood watching the dancing corn all afternoon." *Minky Sloane*